Pokémon™

A New Journey

DK Penguin Random House

Senior Art Editor Anna Formanek
Project Editor Lara Hutcheson
Production Editor Marc Staples
Senior Production Controller Lloyd Robertson
Managing Editor Tori Kosara
Managing Art Editor Jo Connor
Publisher Paula Regan
Managing Director Mark Searle

Designed for DK by Thelma-Jane Robb
Reading Consultant Barbara Marinak

DK would like to thank Hank Woon, Alyssa Tuffey, and the rest of the team at The Pokémon Company International. Thanks also to Julia March for proofreading, and Emma Wicks for design assistance.

First American Edition, 2025
Published in the United States by DK Publishing,
a division of Penguin Random House LLC
1745 Broadway, 20th Floor, New York, NY 10019

25 26 27 28 29 10 9 8 7 6 5 4 3 2 1
001–344848–Feb/2025

Published in Great Britain by Dorling Kindersley Limited

A catalog record for this book is available from the Library of Congress.
ISBN 978-0-5939-5997-8 (Paperback)
ISBN 978-0-5939-5998-5 (Hardcover)

DK books are available at special discounts when purchased in bulk for sales promotions, premiums, fund-raising, or educational use.
For details, contact: DK Publishing Special Markets,
1745 Broadway, 20th Floor, New York, NY 10019
SpecialSales@dk.com

Printed and bound in China

www.dk.com

FSC www.fsc.org MIX Paper | Supporting responsible forestry FSC™ C018179

This book was made with Forest Stewardship Council™ certified paper—one small step in DK's commitment to a sustainable future.
Learn more at www.dk.com/uk/information/sustainability

Level 1

Pokémon™

A New Journey

Julia March

DK

Contents

Sound it out

Try saying these Pokémon names out loud.

Pikachu
[PEE-ka-choo]

Quaxly
[KWACKS-lee]

Sprigatito
[Sprig-uh-TEE-toh]

Ceruledge
[Suh-ROOL-ehj]

Fuecoco
[Fwey-KO-ko]

Black Rayquaza
[Black Ray-KWAY-zuh]

Captain Pikachu

Captain Pikachu is the skilled captain of an airship.

Captain Pikachu

The airship is called
The Brave Olivine.
It travels all over the
Pokémon world.

Friede

Friede is the leader of a group of friends called the Rising Volt Tacklers.

The Rising Volt Tacklers

The friends are going on a new journey. They want to explore the Pokémon world.

Charizard

Charizard is Friede's Pokémon.
They make a great team.

Charizard is very strong in battle. It can use its Flamethrower attack.

The Rising Volt Tacklers

The Rising Volt Tacklers have many talents.

Ludlow loves fishing.

Mollie helps heal injured Pokémon.

Murdock

Orla

Murdock is a great cook.

Orla is good at fixing things.

Pokémon friends

Many helpful Pokémon travel together on *The Brave Olivine*.

Metagross helps Orla with her tasks.

Kind Chansey likes to help Mollie.

Rockruff is often in the ship's kitchen with Murdock.

Dot and Quaxly

Dot is another member of the Rising Volt Tacklers.

Dot can be very secretive.

Quaxly is Dot's Pokémon.
It likes helping Dot make
new friends.

Liko

Liko is a Pokémon Trainer.

Liko owns a pendant that her grandma gave her. She wants to find out its secrets.

Sprigatito

Sprigatito is Liko's Pokémon.
It is a Grass Cat Pokémon.

In battle, Sprigatito can use a move called Leafage.

Amethio

Watch out for Amethio! He is a Pokémon Trainer who wants to steal Liko's pendant.

Amethio's
partner
Pokémon
is called
Ceruledge.

Roy

Meet Roy. He wants to be a top Pokémon Trainer.

Roy hopes to catch the Black Rayquaza. It came out of his Ancient Poké Ball.

Roy's Ancient Poké Ball

Black Rayquaza

Fuecoco

Fuecoco is Roy's Pokémon.

Fuecoco is a Fire Croc Pokémon.
It is cheerful and loves to sing. It loves to eat, too.

Flames

Black Rayquaza

The Black Rayquaza flew away before Roy could catch it.

Roy and Liko
are on an
adventure to
try and find
it again.

Glossary

Partner Pokémon
The Pokémon a Trainer has at the start of their Pokémon journey.

Poké Ball
A ball used by Trainers to catch and carry Pokémon.

Pokémon Trainer
Someone who raises Pokémon and battles with them in competition.

Tera Orb
An item that can cause a Pokémon to become stronger in battle.

Index

Quiz

Ready to find out how much you learned? Read the questions and then check your answers with an adult.

1. What is *The Brave Olivine*?
2. Who is the leader of the Rising Volt Tacklers?
3. Which Pokémon likes to help Mollie?
4. What does Amethio want to steal?
5. Is Fuecoco a Fire Croc Pokémon?

1. An airship 2. Friede 3. Chansey 4. Liko's pendant 5. Yes